The Sky Full Of Unspoken Words

Whispers of the Heart in Silent Verses

Zia Mirza

India | USA | UK

Made with ❤ on the BookLeaf Publishing Platform
www.bookleafpub.in
www.bookleafpub.com

Dedication

To the quiet warriors, the ones who fight battles unseen, carrying storms within yet finding the strength to rise. To the hearts that love despite breaking, to the souls that shine even in darkness—this book is for you.

For every word swallowed, every tear hidden, and every dream feared—these pages hold your voice. You are not weak for feeling deeply, nor broken for carrying pain. Strength is not in silence, but in the courage to keep going.

May these verses remind you that even in your quietest moments, you are heard. Even in your struggles, you are not alone. This book belongs to every soul who has fought in silence—and still chose to rise.

Preface

Some emotions refuse to be spoken, and some stories ache to be told. This book is a collection of those whispers—the silent cries, the quiet victories, the storms and sunrises that live within the heart. Each poem is a fragment of pain and hope, of breaking and healing, of fading and fighting.

We live in a world where vulnerability is often mistaken for weakness, where emotions are silenced and struggles are hidden behind forced smiles. But the truth is—to feel deeply is to be brave. To embrace one's emotions, to acknowledge both joy and sorrow, is an act of strength.

If these words resonate with even one soul, if they bring comfort on a lonely night, then every line has found its purpose. This book is not just mine—it is yours too. It holds the echoes of unspoken thoughts, the weight of untold emotions, and the quiet reassurance that you are not alone.

With every word, may you remember—you are seen, you are heard, and you belong.

Acknowledgements

This book is a journey that was never meant to be walked alone.

I am deeply grateful to the Almighty for blessing me with the strength and inspiration to put my emotions into words.

To my family—your unwavering love has been my foundation, my anchor. You have stood beside me through storms, reminding me that even in darkness, I am never truly lost.

To the friends who held my hand when my own strength faltered—you are the light that kept me going. Your belief in me breathed life into these pages.

To the silent struggles and unseen wounds that shaped these words—I do not curse you, for you have made me who I am.

To every reader who finds a piece of themselves within these lines—thank you. You are why these words matter.

And lastly, to the unspoken—the feelings that were too heavy, the stories that never found their voice—may this book give them wings.

1. The Weight of Almost

I walk a tightrope no one sees,
balancing between "I'm okay" and the abyss.
Some days, I hold steady,
other days, the wind is too strong.

My body is a traitor,
my mind, a battlefield.
Every step is heavy,
every breath, a negotiation.

I smile so they don't ask,
laugh so they don't look too close.
I've learned to bleed quietly,
to swallow my screams like bitter pills.

I disappear in plain sight,
folding into shadows, slipping into silence.
Not because I want to be alone,
but because I don't know how to be seen.

Some nights, the weight is unbearable.
I close my eyes and wonder—
would it be easier to let go?
Would the world notice if I did?

But then, something small holds me here—
a song, a breeze, a stranger's kindness.
The tiniest ember in this dying fire,
just enough to whisper, "Not yet."

So I keep walking,
even when my legs shake,
even when my heart aches,
even when the tightrope cuts into my feet.

I am still here.
Even when no one knows.
Even when it hurts.
I am still here.

2. The Cage of My Own Skin

This body is mine,
yet it moves against me—
a shadow of what it once was.
It carried me through light and laughter,
now it carries only silence,
only ache.

Each step is a struggle,
each breath, a betrayal.
I wear my own skin like a weight,
dragging through days
where no one sees the battle
raging beneath the surface.

How do you explain a war
that leaves no scars to show?
How do you grieve a body
that still breathes
but no longer feels like home?

3. Echoes in My Bones

There is no language
for this kind of pain—
only the heavy quiet,
only the echoes in my bones.

I wake to a fight
that no one can fight for me.
A beast lurks beneath my ribs,
unseen, unheard,
but always there.

I smile, I nod,
I play the part of someone whole.
But beneath the mask,
I am tired—so tired—
of carrying what no one else can hold.

4. A Goodbye Too Soon

At six years old, I left my home,
too young to chase dreams alone.
A tiny heart, a heavy bag,
a goodbye wrapped in love and tags.

Mama smiled, but tears shone through,
Papa said, *"This path's for you."*
I nodded strong, yet deep inside,
I wished I had a place to hide.

No bedtime tales, no arms so wide,
ust empty halls where echoes hide.
Yet in the silence, I held on tight,
to all their hopes, to all their light.

One day, I'll stand where dreams come true,
and say, *"I did this all for you."*

5. A Dream Woven in Love

Before I could spell my name just right,
they saw my future, shining bright.
Before my hands could reach the stars,
they wished for me to go so far.

So, I left home with trembling feet,
a journey unknown, a world to meet.
Nights felt lonely, days were long,
but their love kept me strong.

I read, I learned, I fell, I rose,
grew through every thorn and rose.
Now I stand, their dream in sight—
a story born from love and light.

Because I was never truly alone,
their dream, my wings—I've flown, I've flown.

6. Born of Storms

I was born into storms,
raised by the thunder,
with feet that learned to walk
on roads full of fire.

Every scar is a story,
every wound, a lesson.
I have fallen,
but I have risen—
again and again,
like the sun refusing to stay hidden.

They said the weight would crush me,
that I was too small to fight,
but they never saw
the fire burning in my soul,
the strength stitched into my bones.

7. Forever by My Side

We argue over little things,
who gets the last bite, who sings off-key.
We push, we pull, we roll our eyes,
yet somehow, you still stand by me.

You've seen me stumble, seen me fall,
but never once did you lose faith.
Through every storm, through every doubt,
you cheered for me at every place.

Yes, we fight, and yes, we tease,
but that's just how we show we care.
For in the end, through thick and thin,
I know you'll always be right there.

For siblings aren't just family ties,
they're laughter, trust, and love so true.
And no matter what, through every fall,
I'll always stand right next to you.

8. The Quiet Light

I do not seek the loudest throne,
Nor crave a world to call my own.
I walk unseen, yet leave a trace,
Of kindness wrapped in silent grace.

No need for praise, no need for gold,
My worth is not in stories told.
I bow my head, yet still I rise,
With strength that humbles, never dies.

The loud may fade, the proud may fall,
But gentle hearts outshine them all.
For power whispers, never shouts,
It stands in faith, it lives in doubts.

So judge me not by what you see,
But by the weight of humility.
For in the quiet, soft and true,
Lies all the light that guides me through.

9. Whispers Within

I laugh, I shine, I play my part,
Yet silence lingers in my heart.
No one hears the quiet sigh,
Or sees the tears I blink dry.

The world moves fast, I stand still,
Swallowed whole against my will.
A storm inside, a gentle face,
Lost between time and space.

Maybe one day, light will call,
And break the walls I built so tall.
Till then, I breathe, I wear my guise,
Holding back my weeping skies.

10. Lessons in Letting Go

Whispers turned to knives so cold,
Stories twisted, lies retold.
But every scar upon my skin
Is proof of battles fought within.

I do not mourn what walked away,
The past was never meant to stay.
For every storm, the sun will rise,
And I will heal beneath new skies.

Not every bond is meant to last,
Some belong only to the past.
What is lost has cleared my view,
What remains is strong and true.

11. Rising in a Different Way

I once held stars within my hand,
A child who met each high demand.
Numbers danced, and words would flow,
A mind that shone, a heart aglow.

But life had turns I couldn't see,
Storms that stole the best of me.
The climb grew steep, the path unclear,
Failures whispered in my ear.

Yet, I refused to break or stay,
I rose again—a different way.
Not the same, but stronger still,
With passion forged from iron will.

Now every chance, I hold it tight,
Not chasing past, but new-found light.
For what I lost has paved my way,
And I am proud of who I stay.

12. A Life Worth Living

Do not take this life for granted,
Every breath is love enchanted.
Each sunrise paints a brand-new start,
A lesson stitched into your heart.

The road may twist, the storms may rise,
Tears may fall from weary eyes.
But life does not break you to stay,
It shapes you in a stronger way.

Not the same, but still you grow,
Through every high, through every low.
And when the journey meets its bend,
You'll see—you're shining in the end.

13. The Hands That Held Me

My family—oh, my family, strong,
They held me up when days felt wrong.
Like mountains standing, tall and true,
They faced each storm and pulled me through.

When hands would shake, when hope grew weak,
They gave me strength I couldn't seek.
Through nights of silence, days of pain,
They lit the dark like steady flame.

They saw in me what I had lost,
A soul unbroken, worth the cost.
Not the weak one, not the stray,
But one who'd rise and find their way.

And so I did—not to prove,
Not for those who never knew,
But for the love that stood so tall,
The only voice that meant it all.

14. What's Left is Gold

They laughed when I was weak and worn,
As if my struggle was their scorn.
But sickness did not steal my soul—
It made me fierce, it made me whole.

I lost a few, but found my ground,
No fair-weather hearts around.
What's gone is gone, I will not weep—
I plant my roots, I grow so deep.

Their whispers tried to break my stride,
Yet strength was always on my side.
Each scar, a map of where I've been,
A story inked upon my skin.

I rise with every passing day,
Their shadows fade, but I will stay.
For what remains is pure and true,
And all I lost just cleared my view.

15. Blessings Over Burdens

A lesson learned, a bridge burned,
A world once bright, now overturned.
Yet in the ruins, light remains,
A love untouched by loss or pain.

For every friend who chose to leave,
A kinder soul was sent to me.
So I let go, I stand tall,
What I have is worth it all.

The hands that hurt, the words that stung,
Only made me brave and strong.
No bitterness, no heavy chains,
Just open skies after the rain.

I walk ahead, unburdened, free,
Grateful for what's meant to be.
The past may whisper, but I know,
What's left is gold, and I will glow.

16. My Father's Hands

His hands were worn, his back was bent,
Yet never once did he lament.
Through sleepless nights and endless days,
He lit our world in quiet ways.

He bore the weight so we could rise,
Hid his pain behind his eyes.
No dreams too big, no path too far,
He shaped my life, my guiding star.

The world may never sing his name,
Yet in my heart, it burns like flame.
For every tear he never cried,
A sacrifice he kept inside.

I stand today because he stood,
Giving all he ever could.
No crown, no throne, yet still the best—
A father's love outshines the rest.

17. A Friend Like You

Through every storm, through every fight,
You stood beside me, held me tight.
When shadows fell and hope seemed dim,
You were my light, my trust, my kin.

No whispered doubt, no step behind,
Just endless faith, so pure, so kind.
Through all my highs, through all my lows,
You saw the strength I didn't know.

The world may shift, the seasons change,
Yet one thing stays, never estranged.
A friend like you—so rare, so true,
I stand today because of you.

18. Jannah Lies Beneath Her Feet

She held me close when I was small,
Picked me up from every fall.
Through hungry nights and endless pain,
She bore it all—yet spoke no blame.

Her hands grew worn, her back grew weak,
Yet still, she smiled, too tired to speak.
She wept in prayers I never heard,
Gave up her world to build my world.

She hid her scars behind her grace,
Wiped my tears, but none traced her face.
Her love was fire, fierce and bright,
Burning through each darkest night.

No throne, no crown, no wealth, no name,
Yet Heaven honors her with fame.
For all she gave, for all she weeps,
Jannah lies beneath her feet.

19. Through Every Storm

When shadows fall and doubts arise,
I lift my heart to endless skies.
Through trials fierce and nights so long,
His whisper turns my fear to song.

The road is rough, the path unclear,
Yet faith outshines my every fear.
For every tear, He sends me grace,
In every loss, I find embrace.

No storm can shake what He has planned,
I walk in trust, He holds my hand.
Through rise and fall, through joy and pain,
With Him, my soul will stand again.

So let the winds and tempests call,
I trust His will, He knows it all.
Through every phase, through dark and bright,
The Almighty leads me into light.

20. Rise Again

When shadows creep and doubts arise,
And the world seems deaf to cries,
Stand tall, my friend, don't break, don't bend,
This storm will pass—it's not the end.

They may mock, they may jeer,
Try to drown your voice in fear,
But deep inside, your fire glows,
A spark of hope that only grows.

Not every road is smooth and wide,
Some are steep with pain to hide,
Yet step by step, through trials steep,
Your dreams will wake from where they sleep.

With every fall, rise once more,
Stronger than you were before.
For fate was written, bold and true,
And all this time—it led to you.

21. Grace Unshaken

They spoke in thorns, they broke my trust,
Left my kindness lost in dust.
Yet here I stand, with heart still true,
For hate won't shape what I pursue.

I could return the hurt they gave,
Let anger rise and make me slave,
But vengeance dims the light inside,
And love is where my strength resides.

I'll walk in peace, no chains, no war,
Forgiveness makes my spirit soar.
Not for them, but for my soul,
To rise above, to stay whole.

Let them mock, let them betray,
I won't be lost, I won't decay.
For in the end, it's clear to see,
It's between my Lord and me.

22. Against the Tide

Don't go with the flow, don't drift with the stream,
Rise with your purpose, chase your own dream.
The world may whisper, "Follow the way,"
But your path is yours—don't let them sway.

Waves may push, winds may call,
They want you silent, they want you small.
But stand your ground, don't lose your spark,
A rebel's fire glows in the dark.

Not every road is paved in gold,
Not every story must be retold.
Dare to question, dare to fight,
Forge your truth in fearless light.

So when they ask why you won't bend,
Say, "I walk a road that doesn't end."
For those who dare, for those who try,
Find their wings and learn to fly.

23. A Heart of Gratitude

For every breath, for every day,
For light that guides along my way,
For lessons learned, for love that stays,
I lift my heart in silent praise.

For hands that held me when I fell,
For voices kind with words that swell,
For storms that passed and skies turned blue,
I'm grateful for the old and new.

For strength in trials, hope in pain,
For loss that taught and wisdom gained,
For dreams that grew, for paths made clear,
For every smile, for every tear.

I thank the stars, the earth, the sea,
For all I have, for all to be.
With open arms, I humbly stand,
Grateful for life's gentle hand.

24. The Spark Within

Never doubt, never hide,
There's a spark in you, burning inside.
Not just a whisper, not just a dream,
But a fire alive, a steady gleam.

You may not see it, but it's there,
A force of light beyond compare.
Through darkest nights, through endless fight,
It shines within, fierce and bright.

Don't shrink yourself, don't fade away,
The world needs you in its own way.
Stand up strong, embrace your might,
You are the spark that fuels the light.

25. Beauty Beyond Sight

Everyone shines in their own way,
A light within that won't decay.
Not just the face, not just the skin,
But the soul that glows from deep within.

We chase ideals, we judge, we stare,
Forgetting hearts, forgetting care.
Yet behind each smile, behind each tear,
Lies a story we may never hear.

So let's be kind, let's not break,
A fragile heart for beauty's sake.
For everyone fights battles unknown,
Struggling, healing, on their own.

Let's not be the weight they bear,
But hands that lift, a breath of air.
For beauty isn't just what we see,
It's love, it's kindness—it's you, it's me.

26. Speak with Kindness

Be careful with the words you say,
They linger long, they never stray.
A gentle tone, a heart so true,
Can brighten skies and change the view.

You never know their hidden fight,
The pain they mask, the lonely night.
So speak with love, don't tear apart,
A kind word heals a wounded heart.

For what you give is what you gain,
Harsh words bring nothing but pain.
So spread some warmth, let kindness grow,
A little light will always glow.

27. Lost Without You

Losing you has torn me apart,
A heavy ache within my heart.
The world still moves, but I stand still,
An empty space I cannot fill.

Your voice, once soft, now fades away,
Yet in my dreams, you always stay.
I search for you in fleeting air,
But all I find is pain and prayer.

The chair you loved, the jokes you'd tell,
Echo in the void I know too well.
The warmth you brought, the love you gave,
Now lingers quiet beside your grave.

Some say with time, the grief will fade,
But every day, I feel the same.
I whisper your name to the silent sky,
Asking the heavens—why, oh why?

28. To My Soul

When I was lost in endless night,
You held me close, you shone your light.
Through every tear, through every fall,
You stood beside me through it all.

You heard the cries I couldn't speak,
You held me strong when I was weak.
Through shattered hope and silent screams,
You kept alive my fading dreams.

When all seemed gone, you whispered, **"Fight,"**
You pulled me back into the light.
Oh, soul of mine, so brave, so true,
I stand today because of you.

29. Beyond Power, Beyond Wealth.

Stand up tall, don't look away,
Respect is not for you to weigh.
Not by color, not by creed,
Not by status, wealth, or need.

Every voice and every name,
Burns with fire, shines the same.
No one lesser, no one higher,
We all bleed, we all tire.

Kindness costs you not a dime,
Yet it echoes over time.
Lift them up, don't pull them down,
No one's meant to wear a crown.

Power fades and riches fall,
But the weight of respect is remembered by all.

30. Whispers of the Moon

The midnight air is laced with gold,
soft secrets spun, both new and old.
The stars lean close, they watch, they gleam,
as night unfolds like a lucid dream.

The river hums a lullaby,
reflected worlds drift idly by.
A silver owl calls through the trees,
its echo lost in the midnight breeze.

Not all is seen, not all is known,
some magic breathes where dusk has grown.
So close your eyes, let wonder bloom,
and hear the whispers of the moon.

31. Daughters of Fire

They called us weak, they spoke with doubt,
"Girls can't lead, let men stand out."
But watch us rise, unchained, unbound,
With flames that burn the walls around.

We were not born to beg or kneel,
Our dreams are iron, our souls are steel.
Each scar we wear, each tear we shed,
Fuels the fire they learned to dread.

We build, we break, we shape, we mold,
Turn dust to strength, turn wounds to gold.
No chains can hold, no storm can tame,
The fire within, the untamed flame.

So let them speak, let them sneer,
We are the daughters they learned to fear.
Not just embers, not just sparks,
We are the fire that lights the dark.

32. A Roller Coaster Called Life

I climbed so high, I touched the sky,
Then crashed so hard, I wished to die.
Laughter echoed, wild and free,
Then silence came and swallowed me.

A love so fierce, it lit my soul,
A loss so deep, it left a hole.
One moment, flying—wind so sweet,
The next, I'm begging at life's feet.

Hope embraced me, held me tight,
Then let me go into the night.
I swore I'd rise, I swore I'd fight,
But pain still kissed me every night.

Yet here I stand—scarred but strong,
Still breathing, still singing along.
For every fall, for every climb,
This ride is cruel—this ride is mine.

33. The Unheard Cry

He stands in crowds, yet walks alone,
A weary heart, a soul unknown.
Taught to fight, but not to cry,
To wear a mask, to scrape the sky.

His hands have built, his feet have bled,
Yet words of guilt weigh down his head.
A villain's name, a heavy chain,
For sins not his, yet faced with blame.

He longs to speak, to just be heard,
But silence wraps around his words.
For in this world, where strength must reign,
A man who feels must bear the pain.

34. The Hunger That Never Sleeps

A child wakes to an empty plate,
Dreams swallowed by the hand of fate.
Barefoot streets, the cold winds bite,
Yet hope still flickers in the night.

Hands once soft now rough with toil,
Digging deep in barren soil.
Coins that jingle, never stay,
Spent on hunger, washed away.

Eyes that plead, yet none will see,
A world that thrives on misery.
Palaces rise, while shanties fall,
The rich have much, yet give so small.

Yet poverty is not just lack of bread,
But hearts gone blind, souls left unfed.
A world that turns from those in need,
Will one day choke on its own greed.

35. The Pause That Holds It All

There lies a world so vast, so deep,
Between the beats we barely keep.
A fleeting pause, a breath so still,
Where time bends softly to our will.

It holds the love we couldn't say,
The dreams we lost along the way.
A whispered name, a fleeting glance,
A fate denied its final dance.

It hums with all we left behind,
Regrets that echo through the mind.
Yet in its hush, a truth is spun—
What's meant to be is never done.

For silence speaks where words fall weak,
It mends the cracks we dare not seek.
And in that space so small, so brief,
We find both sorrow—and relief.

36. Between Rain and Rainbow

The rain hums low, a sorrowed sigh,
Grey clouds whisper, veiling the sky.
Each drop that falls, a silent tear,
Washing away what I once held dear.

The wind may howl, the thunder may cry,
Yet storms don't last—they pass us by.
And as the sky begins to glow,
A quiet magic starts to show.

A rainbow arcs, so soft, so bright,
Born from the tears, bathed in light.
For every storm that breaks me down,
A bridge of color will be found.

37. The Pulse of Survival

A heart that beats must ache and break,
Must know the sting, must bear the weight.
For silence comes when all is smooth,
A lifeless pulse, a hollow truth.

The monitor hums in jagged cries,
Rising, falling—pain survives.
For only those who dare to bleed
Will ever know what it means to breathe.

A steady line, a quiet rest,
Is nothing more than death confessed.
No struggle left, no fight to win,
No love to lose, no war within.

So let me suffer, let me fall,
Let sorrow carve me, take it all.
For if I break, I know I live—
A heart that beats has more to give.

38. Hostel Nights and Hollow Hearts

The walls have heard our silent cries,
Midnight whispers, longing sighs.
A bed that knows our restless turns,
A ceiling painted with dreams that burn.

Laughter fades but lingers still,
Loneliness creeps, quiet and chill.
Shared sorrows, untold fears,
Worn-out pillows soaked in tears.

Between goodbyes and starting new,
We lost ourselves, but somehow grew.
And when we leave, we'll always roam
Yet call this place our second home.

39. The forgotten souls

They walk the earth with quiet grace,
A gentle heart, a fearless face.
They do not ask, they do not plead,
Yet give us more than what they need.

Their eyes reflect a world untold,
Of love so pure, so brave, so bold.
Yet hands that should be kind and fair,
Turn to harm, forget to care.

They bleed, they break, yet still they trust,
Even when we've turned to dust.
Oh, hear their cries, so soft, so deep,
A promise made, yet failed to keep.

For all they ask is space to roam,
A world to share, a place called home.
So let us heal what we have scarred,
And love them back with open hearts.

40. The Final Page

And so we reach the closing line,
Yet every word still dares to shine.
The echoes of each thought remain,
Like gentle whispers in the rain.

The ink may dry, the spine may wear,
But stories live beyond despair.
Each tear, each laugh, each silent plea,
A part of you, a part of me.

Through every scar, through every fall,
You've risen, stronger than them all.
This book may end, but not your way,
The journey calls—don't shy away.

So take these words, let them ignite,
A flame that glows beyond the night.
For though the pages close in time,
Your story soars—your soul will climb.